Once Upon A Time From Sicily

By

Carmen Carlson

authorHOUSE™

1663 Liberty Drive, Suite 200
Bloomington, Indiana 47403
(800) 839-8640
www.AuthorHouse.com

© 2005 Carmen Carlson. All Rights Reserved.

No part of this book may be reproduced, stored in a retrieval system, or transmitted by any means without the written permission of the author.

First published by AuthorHouse 12/31/04

ISBN: 1-4184-9080-6 (sc)

Library of Congress Control Number: 2004096065

Printed in the United States of America
Bloomington, Indiana

This book is printed on acid-free paper.

This is a book inspired by my family history; some of the details and characters are fictitious and some very real. I hope you will find yourself lost in the truths and lies that inspired the chronicles of our lives. In this bittersweet story, you will find suspense, drama, death, and hope, with a great deal of love for family and a strong will to survive and someday find each other.

I encourage all of you to do a little bit of searching and to learn more about your own family history. You'll be surprised to find a brand-new story to add to the old one.

For you are a part of who they were ...

—Carmen Carlson

Table of Contents

Chapter I 1

Chapter II 9

Chapter III 23

Chapter IV 33

Chapter V 53

Note: 79

Chapter 1

It all started on a late evening in the month of July. It was a warm night and I could not sleep, so I stayed up watching the late-night shows on TV. As I got up to get a glass of water, the phone rang. I quickly answered it, as I didn't want the kids to wake up. As I said, "Hello?" a voice almost whispering answered by asking me, "What do you want more then anything?" I kept quiet as thoughts rushed through my mind. "Who is this?" I asked. And without any delay, he hung up. I went to the kitchen, and as I poured the water into my glass I could not get the phone call out of my mind. What kind of question was that? Who could it be? Since I could not figure it out, I told myself that it was some kind of terrible joke. Finishing my TV show, I went to bed.

The next day I called my job and asked for the day off. I wasn't feeling well. I think I caught a summer cold from my oldest son, Andrew. Sebastian was already up and watching his morning shows. I told the boys I was staying home and they could too. You cannot imagine how many hugs I got. I consider myself very blessed. I have two wonderful boys, who are my pride and joy. We decided to make it into a family day, staying in our PJ's all day, and when we got hungry I fixed us a big breakfast of pancakes and eggs! Mmm, mmm, mmm. The rest of the day we lay around and played board games and picked on each other, laughing and screwing around. Suddenly the phone rang. I stared at it like I knew it was him. I picked up the phone and answered, "Hello?" His voice was breaking in and out as if he was using a cell phone, and I could not make out what he was saying. But I knew it was him again. I said one more time, "Hello?" Again he asked, statically and breaking away, "What do you want more then anything?" I was getting frustrated, so I raised my voice and said, "Look you! You better stop this nonsense and say what you're calling me for!" Yet there was no answer. I hung up abruptly. The kids got up from the carpet and asked, "Who is it mommy?" Visibly shaken up I answered, "I don't know." Andrew, the oldest, right away took the attitude of the man of the house. "If the phone rings again I'll answer it, Mom." We hugged and went back to playing board games in the living room.

I told the boys what was going on, although I did not want to alarm them. I explained to them that a man with a thick accent kept calling me, asking a question. I wanted them to be aware so that if anyone came to the door or if the phone rang again, they would not let anyone in or give any information out. I keep the boys informed of all things. This way they can be alert and learn to make decisions based on common sense. The rest of the day, we sat around and watched TV, being lazy around the house. All too soon, this wonderful day was over. If there was ever a perfect day with my boys, I would say that this was it. I know the boys are growing up fast. These times are to be treasured by me and believe me, they are. I also know soon they will ask questions about our family, and they will have to know.

The next day we did what we usually do. I got up to go to work, and the boys got up to go to school. I work for three doctors in one office. And there is never a dull moment, I tell you. It's always very busy at work. I'm the acting supervisor. Our regular supervisor is out sick. Indefinitely. I wonder why? Perhaps it's the daily stress of dealing with complaints and all sorts of problems, which would overwhelm anyone. But, away you go. On and on, until the end of the day when you tell yourself as you get into your car, "Thank God! The day is finally over!" I got home around 5:00 p.m. Andrew and Sebastian were already home, doing their homework and waiting for me. The first thing that was said to me as soon as I walked in, of course, was, "Hi, Mom. I'm hungry." I went straight to the kitchen and started supper. I put the soup on the stove so it would begin to cook and went to get the mail. Halfway to the door, the phone rang and reluctantly I picked up the receiver. It was just my mother. We talked for a minute or two and then I told her I had dinner on the stove and that I would call her later. We said our goodbyes and then hung up. As I attempted to pick up the mail again, I heard the soup on the stove boiling over. I hurried back to the kitchen and lowered the fire. Finally I was able to get the mail and look through it. Of course, there were bills and newspaper ads. But there was also a small, white envelope addressed to me, with no stamp and no return address. I thought it was a little odd, but there was a fight about to break out. So I put everything on the table and refereed. Soon after that, dinner was ready so we sat down to eat. While we ate, we talked about our day. This helps us to keep connected to one another.

Everyone has a job in this house. The boys' job after dinner is to pick up the table. They pile up the dishes on the sink for me to wash. Then they finish their homework or take out the trash, and afterward we all dry the dishes together and put them away. This time after they picked up the table they both had to finish their homework, so they moved all of my mail to a table in the living room. While washing the dishes, I heard them talking about their friends and TV shows, arguing about which one of them is the best. Boy! What a dilemma life is for young boys. We love our small family. We called ourselves The Three Musketeers: "One for all, and all for one!"

Time to go to bed always came fast for the boys. Listening to their daily complaints is so funny. "But I'm not sleepy, Mom? Can I stay up just a little bit it longer? Please?" Or in a last-ditch effort to steal just a couple of more minutes, "But I forgot to brush my teeth." It always takes a few minutes to settle them in and put them to bed. Then we pray together, we hug, and as I leave the room we blow kisses to each other. Then our day is done.

This night we had a summer storm. It was raining and windy. The hallway was semi-dark, and the tree branches softly hitting the windows around the house reminded me of a mystery novel. I quietly gathered my stuff and went to take a bath. As I tiptoed through the hallway into the bathroom, I suddenly craved a hot cup of tea to sip while I took my bath. I absolutely love English tea with lots of sugar and milk. Putting my things down on the bathroom counter, my eyes caught the reflection of my face in the mirror. Oh! How the years had gone by leaving their marks. The sleepless nights worrying about bills, the boys, and Mom. I caught myself daydreaming and snapped out of it. I went to the kitchen to make my cup of tea. Sitting down at the table, waiting for my water to boil, I remembered I had not yet opened the mail. I picked up the odd letter and began to open it when I heard Andrew coughing. I set the letter down, grabbed a spoon, and went to the medicine cabinet to get the cough medicine. After I gave Andrew some of it, I whispered in his ear, "Sleep well, my son." I played with his hair until he fell asleep again. I returned to the kitchen and made my tea. And, finally submerged into my hot bath, leaving the cares of the day behind, the day was really over this time.

Thank God the weekend was finally here. Saturday morning we all get to sleep in. When the kids wake up, they climb in bed with me and we plan our day together while tickling one another. Once we get the chores around the house done, which is usually by early afternoon, we call the kids' friends in the neighborhood and play pool in the garage. We make up teams and play for sodas and candy. None of us really know the rules to pool, so we cheat and argue like pros. It's a lot of fun. We have a small budget in this house but I always make sure the kids are taken care of, the bills are paid, and ultimately that we have fun! Sundays we all go to church. This particular Sunday, Mom decided to go to her Spanish church, so after church the boys and I grabbed a bite to eat and went straight home. Mom is the only family we have left. To the boys and me, she is our world. We have always leaned on each other, Mom and I.

But I understand that sometimes she needs to get away and be with people her own age.

My life is pretty simple. No mysteries or dramas. All of that was left behind a long time ago. Or so I thought. My life consists of my God, my kids, Mom, and work. Sometimes I'll go out with my girlfriends to dinner or dancing. Little did I know my life was about to change direction and even zip code really soon.

Sunday evening, sitting around the kitchen table after dinner, the boys asked me about our relatives. They asked how come they have no grandfathers and only one grandma. And no cousins or aunties. I answered, "Let's make some hot English tea with lots of sugar and milk and I'll bake us some cookies too." *And then I will let you know what I decide; this will give me time to think,* I thought to myself. As I baked and gathered my thoughts, I made up my mind. I was going to tell them. They were getting older and they needed to know and understand who they are in the scheme of life. We got our tea and cookies and went into the living room. I could feel the anticipation of the moment in the air. You could also see it in their eyes. They new this was a guarded subject. I took a deep breath and said to the boys, "We are going to take a trip into our legacy, and it is going to be bittersweet. We come from a big scheme of mysteries. The knowledge of where we came from and what it took to get here comes with responsibilities. Some things are not so good, but our ancestors felt they needed to be done. Secrets and mysteries. Adventures and mishaps. They all pile up and fill the cooking pot of our life. You're going to find out things that are a bit scary, and also treasures of love and warm hearts. Some people were not too good and others very good and kind. But in all, I want you boys to understand that the most important thing in this life is family. Blood. You understand?" I asked. They both nodded their heads and stared quietly. "Promise you will not repeat anything said here tonight. This is not a joke." They both said, "We promise, Mommy. We promise!" The anticipation was building up. I could see it in their faces. Then I took a sip of my tea and a bite of my cookie. They both did the same. Without anymore delays, I began to tell them first about my father's family.

Chapter II

As I began to tell them the story, our minds traveled back in time to the first episodes of how we came to be. When I closed my eyes as I spoke, I could feel myself being right there with everyone. Living and breathing the same air. Hoping and praying. Dreaming and carrying on....

"Grandpa Carlo's family is Sicilian. Full-blooded Sicilians. His story is filled with unfavorable circumstances, hard work, Mafia assassins, identity changes, and more." The boys brought pillows down from the couch and put their drinks aside. They got comfortable and their little eyes were set on me, in full attention as I continued.

There were two brothers that came from Sicily in the early 1900s. They were very young when they had to leave all they knew and loved to hide in Monterrey, Mexico. Carlo, your great grandfather, losing no time, found a job and worked day and night to provide for Giovanni, his younger brother. He went without, saving every penny. Soon he had enough to buy small things and resell them. He did that for a while, and then he opened a small store. He was open twenty-four hours a day. I think this may have been the first twenty-four-hour store. The store got so big that soon he had his own warehouse. As soon as he could, he enrolled Giovanni in a private school. He hoped for Giovanni to become a gentleman. Well mannered and studied. The boys grew up into manhood; they were both handsome and smart. Carlo was thin, tall, and olive skinned, with beautiful brown eyes. He turned heads when he walked into a room. There was an air about him. He was an honest, hard-working man, and his reputation followed him everywhere. He was well liked and respected. Giovanni was not as tall, but also olive skinned, with wavy black hair and a sweet baby face. He was a free-spirited young man and a jokester.

Years went by and they kept themselves busy and got noticed by society, established rich families, and began to invite them to socials and dinners. The two brothers were quite the desirable pair< as young, successful, handsome European men were not in abundance in these parts. As you can imagine, they were pretty popular. Families began to give parties in their honor to help them look for wives. They knew it all along and played the part. Everyone wanted to set them up, and then, of course, brag about it.

It was at a Christmas party, I believe, when Carlo's eyes encountered Sofia's. She was beautiful and elegant, of small stature, with long brown hair that lay carelessly around her head. Her eyes were like jadestone and her lips small and inviting. To bring his brother out of a coma, Giovanni shook his arm and said in Italian, "She is almost as beautiful as a Sicilian girl." He then walked away with his friends, making fun of Carlo. But Carlo didn't care. Sofia stared at Carlo only for a minute, but it was long enough to make his heart stop and take his breath away. She then smiled at him and went on up the stairs with her friends, giggling and whispering. Carlo thought he was going to die when he lost sight of her. Then the men begin to withdraw into the study room, where they smoked cigars and talked business. He was being dragged in, but needless to say he could only think of the beautiful young girl who had just captured him.

The next day he inquired about this girl. He learned her name was Sofia and that she just returned from and all-girls school in England. More importantly she was single and not engaged to anyone. He was beside himself with happiness. He kept repeating her name day and night, until one night Giovanni yelled from his room, "Enough! Marry the girl!" Carlo took his advice and he spoke with her family and asked permission to see her. They gladly agreed, and Sofia and Carlo met. Carlo began to shower her parents with presents from all over the world to win their consent for marriage. Soon weeding plans began. The two were so in love they could hardly wait to marry. When the wedding day arrived, and what a wonderful day this was, everyone was cheerful and happy. Carlo could hardly sleep the night before. He reminisced about his mother and the circumstances that brought them to this place so far away from home. He wished his mother could attend the weeding and be part of his happiness. But he knew this was impossible. He would never see his mother or kiss her forehead again. He would never smell the ocean in the early mornings or take a deep breath of that Sicilian air. Putting his head down, he prayed and asked for her blessing in his marriage. It must have been early morning when he finally went to bed.

The next day he opened his eyes to the loud, exciting voice of his brother Giovanni. He was jumping on his bed and messing up his hair. "Get up! Get up!" Giovanni yelled. "You have got to get on your penguin suit." Words were exchanged in Italian and Spanish. "Come on and have some bread and wine with me, brother, before the chain goes around your neck forever!" Pushing him and laughing, Giovanni went on. They both got ready and walked down the stairs side by side. Carlo put his hand on Giovanni's shoulder and said, "This is the happiest moment of my life, brother, and I have you as my best man by my side."

Sofia was as nervous as any young bride. Upset stomach and all, she was running around, and running around after her were all the servants. It was such a funny site. She was so excited and nervous. But somehow her hair got done and she put on her wedding dress with her flowers in hand and finally, she was ready. When it was announced that she was ready to come down, excitement filled the rooms of the house. "Everyone!" shouted her mom. "Come here! Come on. Sofia is coming down!" All of the servants rounded up to see Miss Sofia as a bride. Upstairs in Sofia's room, her dad stared at his lovely young daughter. Putting his arm out for her to grab, he asked, "Are you ready my child?" She took a deep breath and answered, "Yes!" The dress was gorgeous. There was not another one like it. It was brought all the way from New York. The flowers in her hands were red roses with ribbons intertwined. She had a crown with pearls and diamonds hanging all around it. She looked stunning. She had the sparkle in her eyes of a young girl ready to embrace a new life as a wife and ready to become a woman.

As she appeared and began to come down the round stairs, you could hear the oohs and the aahs from everyone. Sofia's mother looked up and with teary eyes said to her, "My dearest, if only I could stop time, I would stop this moment forever. You look beautiful, my child." Sofia was not the only one decked out for the occasion. The church was all dressed up too, with flowers and candles illuminating the path to the cross, where their marriage would be blessed and their commitment recorded in God's presence. The ceremony was beautiful. There wasn't a dry eye in the entire cathedral. Even the priest had teary eyes. He had known Sofia from the time she was born and baptized by him. He also knew this couple was truly in love and deserving of each other. Little did they know it wouldn't be long before tragedy and suffering would strike their happiness and destroy this beautiful romance, tearing families apart.

The party was amazing. Newspaper reporters came from all over to write about this exclusive wedding. All of the ladies showed off, wearing elegant dresses and colorful jewelry. In one hand the gentlemen had a Cuban cigar, and in the other imported cognac. The ballroom was overflowing with flowers, candles, and ribbons. The orchestra played soft music in the background, and the tables were packed with all sorts of food. The cake was enormous and decorated with flowers made of sugar. Everything was perfect. Just like Carlo and Sofia's love. They danced the night away until midnight when they said their goodbyes and left for their honeymoon in El Capitan, the best cruise in all Mexico. Carlo kissed his brother goodbye and in Italian whispered in his ear, "Be careful. And keep an eye on the business. But don't let your studies go. We need a doctor in the family." They smiled at each other and the honeymooners left.

Two weeks went by, and Giovanni was diligent with both the business and his studies. He worked day and night to keep himself busy. He missed Carlo so much; after all, he was his only family. He had his mind made up not to let his brother down with school or the business. One afternoon as he was standing by the big window in his office, watching the crowds of people come in and go out of the warehouse gates, his mind went wandering back to his childhood. He remembered growing up in the house he now missed so much. His family was poor, but his mom always managed to cook delicious meals. He remembered how his father was an honest, hard-working man, yet life never seemed to give him a break. He tried to recall that night they left. It all happened so fast. He was so young. In his memory, there were only bits and pieces of how it happened. But he definitely remembered why they had to leave and how his father died. But what about his mother? Could she still be alive, living with relatives? How old would she be now? Tears ran down his cheeks. He knew he would never see her again. His heart felt like it was breaking in tiny little pieces again and there was nothing he could do. He walked away from the window. Wiping his tears, he poured himself a drink. Still in deep thought, he heard a knock on the door. It was the mail carrier bringing in a letter. Giovanni signed for it and read the postmark. It was from Carlo and Sofia. He tipped the man and closed the door behind him. Opening the letter he began to read. It was a simple letter, which began with salutations. They spoke of how happy they were and how much fun they were having. The letter stated that they would return the following Wednesday. Carlo had to be there to close a deal with some foreign vendor. Giovanni was to pick them up. The letter ended saying, "When we return, there is something we must tell you!" Giovanni wondered what it was they needed to tell him and why they couldn't tell him in their letter. He thought that perhaps they were going to tell him he needed to move out. Or possibly they were going to be moving out themselves. But all he knew was as long as they were coming back, that's all that mattered. Everything else would work out. He missed his brother terribly. Giovanni was genuinely happy for his brother. He knew if anyone deserved happiness it was Carlo. He had never forgotten all the sacrifices his brother had made for him. It was time he had some happiness of his own.

The day came for Giovanni to pick them up. Being so excited, he was bright and early. He brought flowers for Sofia and a big hug for his brother. He had missed them so much. As soon as they got home, Carlo began telling Giovanni what it was he needed to tell him. He told Giovanni about the changes that were going to take place since they had married. He said, with Sofia by his side, "My dear brother," gesturing with his hand for Giovanni to sit down. As he did so, Giovanni's heart skipped a heartbeat. "Sofia and I have been thinking that this house is big enough for all of us. And I hate to leave you alone; after all, we are Sicilians and brothers. We don't leave each other behind." Giovanni's day was made. He was elated that they decided to stay! Leaping out of his seat, he hugged them both. Then Carlo put one arm around his brother and the other around Sofia. "All right! So it's settled. We all can live together as a family. Let's get unpacked." Carlo went back to running the business full speed and Giovanni to his studies. Sofia had the biggest task of all. She had to put a woman's touch in the house. Boy did she need to shop.

Three months passed by, when over breakfast Sofia declared, "I can not eat! Food makes me sick!" Carlo and Giovanni looked at each other, confused. Carlo said, "Dear, maybe we can get another cook?" Giovanni made the suggestion for her to try some toast and black tea to settle her stomach. "I don't think tea and toast will take care of my problem," she said. With a big smile she announced, "I'm with child!" It took Carlo and Giovanni a few seconds to catch on to what she had just said. Looking at each other, they got up and ran toward her. Carlo lifted her up above his shoulders and twirled her around. Round and round the room they went, laughing and kissing. Giovanni hung on to both of them, screaming, "I'm going to be an uncle!" The servants came running from every direction to find out what the disturbance was. This was indeed a happy day for this family of three, soon to be four!

Her parents and friends were notified right away. Carlo's in-laws were euphoric hearing the good news. Plans for a baby shower began to spark. It was the talk of the town. Sofia and Carlo were the happiest couple in the world. They began to call for decorators for the baby's new nursery. It had to be blue. After all, according to Carlo it was going to be a boy. Furniture was ordered immediately. Dreams and excitement filled the house. Two weeks later, Giovanni graduated from medical school. I don't think Carlo could have been any more proud of his little brother. There was finally a doctor in the family. A garden party was given in his honor, following the ceremony. Half of the town came to the party, where they danced, ate, and celebrated with the two brothers and a very pregnant Sofia!

The following day was a Sunday. Carlo wanted to surprise his brother and buy a small building for him to open his own practice in. He was going to stay in the office at his house all day, working on plans for his brother's surprise. Sofia had planned to spend the afternoon with her mother. Giovanni didn't waste any time. It was his first day at the city hospital. He was officially a doctor. They all planned to have dinner together as usual around six o'clock. Carlo worked on the tasks at hand for hours, until his shoulders got so tired he had no choice but to get up and stretch his arms. He walked around the room, where he noticed the time. It was almost five o'clock. He dashed up the stairs to take a quick shower. He climbed in the shower and allowed the water to fall down on his tired shoulders. As he finished soaping his face, he heard the bathroom door open. With his soapy eyes closed, he called out, "Sofia? Come on in and join me. The water is great!" But there was no answer. He said again, "Darling! Come in. Don't be shy. I won't hurt my little pumpkin," he said playfully. Still there was no answer. He reached for his towel and it was handed to him. Wiping his face, he opened his eyes and saw who it was: Salvatore, his old friend from Sicily, holding a gun and looking down as with shame. Carlo calmly said, "I understand, but it ends right here, my friend. With me." Salvatore answered, "Sí." Carlo could hardly finish his last sentence. "I forgive you, my friend," when one shot was fired directly at his heart. His body fell to the ground. Water was still running as his blood ran down the drain. Innocent blood. There was no one home. Carlo, our dear Carlo, died alone. It didn't matter if it was right or wrong, but it had to be done in order to save someone's honor back home. Mr. Santini ordered it. This is how business was done.

Sofia got home at around five thirty in the afternoon. She opened the door and yelled for Carlo to help her with the packages she was carrying. But no one came to help. Putting the packages down, she began to climb the stairs. Giovanni stepped in front of her and stopped her. She playfully said to him, "Step aside, you gorilla. I'm looking for my husband!" Sofia tried to push him aside, but he wouldn't move. He softly grabbed her arms and said, "Sofi, don't go upstairs." She looked up and saw his face was pale and that he had tears rolling down his cheeks. She knew immediately something was wrong. "Get out of my way!" she said. She screamed for Carlo, but no one came. Pleading with her, Giovanni continued to beg her not to go upstairs. "Think of the baby!" he said. She screamed, "No! I want Carlo!" once more calling for Carlo to come. "Let me go!" she argued. Still trying to push him aside, Giovanni finally gave up and let her through. Up the stairs she went, calling for Carlo and looking in every room she passed. Finally, there were no more screams for Carlo; she found her beloved Carlo on the shower floor. She dropped to her knees and ever so carefully caressed Carlo, laying him in her lap. She told him to wake up. First softly, and as he would not respond, she started shaking him, screaming to him to stop playing and wake up. Shock and denial filled her mind. Giovanni entered and tried to take her away, but she would not let go of her Carlo. He tried to reason with her. "He's gone, Sofi," he said. "He's gone." She was crying hysterically, screaming at him. "Don't give up on your brother so easily! He never gave up on you! Do something!" Giovanni answered her saying, "He's gone Sofi. There's nothing I can do." Covering his face with his hands, he wept bitterly. Sofia's body could not take it any longer and gave up. She fainted over her beloved Carlo's lifeless body.

Giovanni called the police and the hospital. Everyone was in shock as the news circulated quickly throughout the town. There were reporters and friends of the family in every corner of the house. Giovanni asked Sofia's parents to stay upstairs with her to protect her from all of this. When everyone was finally gone, he went upstairs to talk to Sofia. She was still numb, sitting at the edge of the bed. He politely asked her parents to leave them alone and they did. He told Sofia, "I don't have time to explain the whys, but I can tell you this: you're in danger, Sofi. You and the baby." Shaking her, he told her, "Snap out of it. Sofia, they have found us. If you have a boy, they will take his life too!" Sofia asked softly, "Who are they?" She did not understand what he was talking about. He shook her again, "Sofia! You must get out of here right away!" Giving her a suitcase full of cash, Giovanni told her, "I will have Eduardo escort you to the train station. Go and disappear. I don't want to know where you're going. Look for me two years from now in Los Angeles, California. I will be at the Beverly Hills Hotel on the same date as today. Sofia, two years from now. Don't forget!" Softly pushing her down the stairs and out the door, he made her leave. Giovanni sank into a chair and begin to cry again. Carlo was gone. His only brother. Now Sofia and the baby must leave too. He was all alone.

Sofia arrived in Mexico City exhausted from sleepless nights. She still did not understand what had happened, but she promised her still-unborn child that she would find out someday. Sofia told herself that she needed to be strong for the baby. She began to plan her life. First, she decided that she and the baby needed a house and a couple of servants to help them out. "I will go to the municipio (hall of records) and claim someone stole my papers. I'll keep my first name, but I'll change our last name," she said to her baby, rubbing her stomach. "This way, my little one, once you are born, you'll have another identity all together. Then I need to think, think hard—what kind of business I can open for us?" Sofia decided she new only one business and that was retail.

Sofia soon gave birth to a baby boy whom she named Carlitos. After the baby's birth, she opened a small warehouse to at first test the waters. But no one would do business with a woman. She was treated like a second-class citizen and was constantly engaged in battles. She battled and fought with vendors, buyers, employees, you name it. The first problem was that she was a young woman and had a child. Secondly, she had no support and couldn't talk to or involve her family back home. She was totally alone. The women gossiped about her constantly, and the men would pay no attention to her attempts to do business with them. She needed to earn their respect, and that is next to impossible. Sofia worked day and night to make her business succeed. And finally it did. It took off, but took about two years for her to see results. Finally everything fell into place. Her doors were open and the business was booming. Still very angry with Giovanni for not explaining things to her and upset over her husband's death, she never went to Los Angeles to meet him. Furthermore, she had no time for him with her business thriving as well as it was. Giovanni, however, was there waiting for Sofia. He waited there for her for a month, yet she never showed. He finally gave up and went back home.

Being alone made Sofia a strong woman. But it also made her grow a very thick skin, and she became mean, spiteful, and hateful to all. To everyone except Carlitos. Her beloved baby had all her love. She made sure Carlitos attended the crème de la crème of private schools. He had two nannies and a butler to take care of all his needs. Nothing but the best would do for her son. He was a smart little boy and very charming. As Carlitos got older, Sofia began to worry about how people would treat him with no father by his side. Sofia made a very difficult decision and decided that she needed to wed and soon. She thought, *I will look for someone powerful; so powerful everyone will respect my son and me. I will look for him with my mind not my heart.* Sofia was a vibrant and beautiful young woman, and smart too; she knew that she would have no problem finding a husband. With tears in her eyes, she forced herself to write the invitations to a gala affair. There were bets among men who would win her heart. She had made for herself a reputation of being cold-hearted, but she was beautiful, young, and very rich. Who wouldn't want to marry such a girl?

When the day came, there were flower arrangements in every corner of the house, giving the air a sweet smell. The sparkles of the chandeliers made a splash on the walls in colorful displays as you entered the room. The champagne flowed freely down from a cascade made of ice. The orchestra was the best in all of Mexico City. When Sofia entered the room, everyone gasped. She of course looked stunning as always. She danced the night away with all of the available men, young and old alike. She chose an older general to be her husband and father figure to her son. He was a powerful man. He was second in command under the president of Mexico. Although the general was her senior by many years, he was powerful. And that is what she wanted. "He will do," she told herself as she accepted his proposal for marriage. They wed in a small ceremony right away.

Carlitos was never told about his father or his family. Sofia wanted to erase his past and wanted to make sure nobody could ever find him. After a while she believed she had no family. She never went back to see them. It was said that her mother took her last breath saying her long lost daughter's name, and her father died right after.

Coming out of a mesmerized awe of such a dramatic history of their family, Sebastian interrupted, "So, Mommy, that's how Grandpa's daddy died, but when did Grandpa and Grandma meet?" he asked. "Hold your horses, boy. We have a lot to cover before that. I will tell you soon, but before that we need to talk about Grandma's family too." Andrew smacked his brother on the leg and said, "Be quiet! Let Mom finish!" Before an argument could break out, I began telling them about their grandma.

Chapter III

Mom did not know either one of her parents. Her mother, my grandma Emma, was of Scottish and English descent and her dad was Sicilian. Emma had long, wavy, blonde hair; her eyes, like mine, were hazel; and she had rosy cheeks and a killer smile like Grandma's. Emma was only fifteen years old when she was forced to marry an older German man who was senior by forty years. Her family owned and inn, where he was staying while waiting for a boat to come to America. Emma's family had many children, of whom she was the eldest. Being so, she helped around the inn most of the time. That is where they met. He offered a lot of money for her and they wed. He brought Emma to California and got a job working for the train company as a locomotive engineer. He was gone most of the time, but when he was home, he was drunk and used to take all his frustrations out on her. He was a bitter old man. Emma wasn't allowed to have any friends and he kept her far away from everyone she ever knew and loved. She was always alone. Emma was often left without any money or food, and she couldn't even pay the rent for the room they lived in. But like Sofia, she was a survivor and she was not going to allow her kids to become homeless. Emma arrived at an idea that she would ask the owner of the building she lived in if she could manage it. She told them of her experience of running the inn back home. In exchange for her work, all she wanted was to live there rent-free in a two-bedroom apartment. The owners, who were getting older, liked the idea of letting someone else care for the building. So they agreed and gave her the job and the upgrade to a larger apartment. Emma was beginning to take control of her life and the lives of her children. She was growing up. The next problem to solve was money. If only she could get a job to bring in the money to feed herself and her children. Talking with Maria, her only friend, whom she had kept a secret from her husband, they came up with a plan. Maria was going to look after the children after she got off work, and Emma would search for a job in the evenings. During this time, Emma and Maria became very close. They were both alone in California. Emma was constantly worried about her kids, but Maria promised her that she would take care of them as if they were her own. "Go out and get your job; you have a world to conquer. They'll be fine with me. I promise," Maria told her friend, pushing her out the door. Sad to imagine that one day, Emma's blood would call on Maria's promise.

Emma came home excited. She got a job as a hostess in a prestigious Italian restaurant in Beverly Hills. "I'll be wearing a uniform, sitting people down, and taking reservations. If I wanted some of the leftovers at the end of the night, I can help out cleaning up the kitchen. I'll make money and bring home food too. Isn't this great?" she told Maria. That night Emma made it a point to get on her knees with her kids and pray, thanking God for her new life.

It didn't take long for the owner of the restaurant to notice Emma, who was nineteen now. Angelo was his name. He was a kind Sicilian man in his mid-twenties and everyone liked him. Angelo was a very busy man with his restaurant and was somewhat of a loner. He never had time for a life for himself. His business was very successful now, and he had worked very hard to get to where he was. He came from a small town in Sicily to make a better life for his family back home. When he arrived here with the little money everyone back home had raised for him, he built himself a stand on wheels, where he sold his delicious sausages, cappuccinos, and fruit. He was a hit! He built such a huge clientele that he was able to move into the corner restaurant on Hill Street. It was a modest restaurant, but, nevertheless, his first restaurant. There he continued to succeed making sandwiches, pizza, pastas, and, of course, his delicious sausages. As time went by, he needed a bigger place. That's when he really went for broke and opened the restaurant in Beverly Hills. He put it all on the line and borrowed from wherever he could. He worked hard and made it to the top for everyone back home. As soon as he could, he bought his parents a beautiful villa in their hometown. He made sure they were comfortable and had no needs. He sent each of his brothers money according to their needs and professions. To the oldest he sent enough money for fishing boats and helpers—he was a fisherman—and to the youngest, money for lumber and enough to open a small furniture store in town. Soon his task was done; everyone was taken care of, but he was still alone.

The first time Emma met Angelo, it was at the end of her shift. She had just finished helping to clean the kitchen; as she was washing her hands Angelo passed by and they made light conversation. It was then that she felt butterflies for the first time in her life. Little did she know Angelo did too. This was a foreign feeling for both of them. These two young souls, who had struggled in life and put their own needs aside for others, finally had found a feeling of their own. It was obvious there was a spark between them, but aware of Emma's situation, their behavior remained very proper. The next day Emma was walking on clouds, but she was aware that if her German husband found out she had feelings for Angelo she would be dead in an instant. She only confided in her friend Maria.

One evening as the restaurant was closing down for the night, Emma picked up her belongings and, getting ready to leave, she noticed Angelo. She thought to herself how strikingly handsome he looked in his tuxedo as he begin to slowly walk toward her. Emma's heart was coming out of her chest it was beating so fast. Angelo looked at Emma and said, "Everyone is gone," as he grabbed for her hands and kissed them both. They were both shaking, their eyes fixed on each other. The lights were dim and the music was softly playing in the background. They held hands. Neither one could speak. He touched her face and she his. It was then that they first kissed. With teary eyes they both gazed at each other and embraced. No need to talk; this moment in time was theirs.

Emma worked hard to give her children everything they needed. Angelo helped her by giving her small bonuses here and there. She was proud and did not take any money from him unless she worked for it. No one questioned anything Emma did, but instead were happy for her. Everyone knew that she was making a better life for her children. Christmas Eve came and they all went to church. Angelo and Emma saw each other at the steps. He tipped his hat to her, she smiled, and the kids waved. This night, he realized how alone he was without them. He sat at his dinner table with a bounty of food in front of him, yet there was no one to share a bite, a smile, or a gift. He knew that he missed Emma and the kids so much. He knew the kids from when Emma would bring her children to see him on her days off. They liked him and knew him as "Mommy's nice boss." He envisioned the kids running around the Christmas tree, ripping open presents, and as they discovered toys, new clothing, cookies, and chocolates they would jump for joy! As he went to bed, he prayed for the Lord to keep them safe.

Emma and Angelo secretly loved each other. Although they both wanted to share their happiness with everyone, they were in a compromised position. She was a married women and he was her boss. Angelo constantly begged her to get a divorce and marry him, but Emma knew she would never get a divorce from her husband. He would kill her first, and her kids—what would they grow up to think of her? Angelo continued to beg her, to no avail. Soon Emma was obviously pregnant. Everyone congratulated her at work, not knowing the facts; it was a bittersweet happiness for both of them. While the kids were across the street at the park, playing with their new toys, Emma's husband returned home after one of his long departures. To his surprise he found Emma pregnant. He was furious and began beat her. For her unborn baby's sake, she cried and begged him to stop. She vowed that she would leave, but he had a violent temper and, as drunk as he was, he freely displayed it on her. He beat her to a pulp and he only stopped when her water broke. She went into labor. It was then that Emma gave birth to my mother. She laid in a puddle of blood with her newborn baby girl by her side and tears falling down her cheeks. Her words were only a whisper as life began to leave her. "My precious little one," she said faintly. And then there was one last breath and she was gone. Emma had died.

Maria had heard the commotion from her apartment next door. She couldn't help but hear the begging and the crying but she did not dare come to her rescue. Maria and everyone were afraid of Emma's big, burly husband. Maria cried for her friend, who was just on the other side of the wall; she knew what danger she was in. Then for a minute or two, everything when silent. A baby cried here and there, and there was a knock on her door. It was Emma's husband. He said, "Emma needs you," and turned and left. Maria ran to aid Emma, finding her dead and covered in blood with her naked newborn by her side. Maria quickly picked up the baby and cleaned her up. She then held the baby in her arms and cried for the loss of a dear friend and a mom.

The very next day, Angelo quickly became aware that Emma was running late. He suddenly felt something was wrong. He waited in his office, where he received a note. He read it and almost fell down. He grabbed a chair and fell into it. The words, which he just read, scrambled in his mind. He could not believe what he was reading. The note was only a few words long, but it broke his heart forever.

As Angelo sat and tears filled his eyes, he read the note again: "You stupid fool. You thought you could have her. She is dead and so is your child. You will never find out were I laid them. This is your punishment. From me to you." Angelo sat there for hours in agony. He contemplated many things. But he saw no other option. He had made up his mind. He had had enough of big city life. He had to go back home, right away. It was that day that he deeded his restaurant to the head waitress.

Emma's husband came back and told Maria, "If you want the baby to live, you'll have to care for it. If I keep it I would just beat her or leave her on the street." That was the last time Maria saw Emma's husband. He took his children and left town. Nobody knows where they went. Maria's first thought was to give the baby to Angelo. She went the next day to look for him. When she got there, she noticed something different. She asked to see the owner and was pointed to a woman. She said, "No! No! I need to see Angelo!" She was told that he had sold the restaurant, but perhaps she might be able to catch him in his office in the back. He was there picking up the last of his things. She went through the kitchen to the back and knocked on his door, but she heard the backdoor exit closing. Maria rushed to see if it was Angelo, but all she saw was the back of the taxi taking off. She ran after the taxi, yelling for Angelo, with the baby in her arms. But the taxi never stopped. He never heard her and never looked back, leaving his child behind. Maria ran and ran, but finally stopped after she ran out of breath. Gasping, she said to the baby, "I guess you're meant to be with me." Kissing the baby's, forehead she said, "I will call you, Carmelita, and you will be my little angel without wings." Soon after, Maria left the big city as well. She went back to Mexico City to live with her aunties, and she took baby Carmelita with her.

Maria went on to begin a new life in Mexico. She married and raised her own family, and always kept an eye on Carmelita. Maria's aunties Lola and Anita loved the baby and helped raise her in a loving home as their own. Carmelita grew up and knew nothing of her family; although I'm sure there where times were she must have asked herself where her mom and dad were, she never asked Maria. I guess she was afraid of the answer. She was a happy child; she was loved and cared for. Carmelita looked like a doll with her curly, blonde hair and her rosy cheeks. Unfortunately, school was not Mom's cup of tea. She liked helping her aunties better, so she stopped going to school around fifth grade and begin to help around the restaurant Lola and Anita owned. It was a taqueria, or taco stand. It was there that she took orders, washed dishes, took out trash, and cleaned tables. She made good tips and saved every penny in case one day she wanted to go back to school or do something with her life.

When Carmelita was sixteen years old, she got tired of working for her aunts and wanted her own business. She asked Mr. Ortiz, the neighborhood carpenter, to build her a cart with wheels where she could sell flowers. It was then that Carmelita would get up early in the morning and go buy the prettiest flowers she could find. She taught herself how to make flower arrangements, and she actually got pretty good at it. She sold the flower arrangements at the prestigious University of Mexico. She knew the rich young men would spend money on her pretty flowers to impress the girls, and she was right; she made a lot of money and had good business there.

She may have been an unwanted child by circumstance, a lost child by fate, a love child by choice. But she was blessed with beauty and kindness and she is my mother.

Chapter IV

Father was tall and olive skinned, with black hair and brown eyes. He was just like his father Carlo. He was also friendly and kind to others, well liked and rich, very rich. "To answer your question earlier, Sebastian, I'm about to tell you how Grandpa and Grandma finally met."

Like Uncle Giovanni, father loved medicine too. He took classes at the University of Mexico. One day as Carlos got out of class, he and his friends were walking across campus, and between his friends' heads Carlos saw an angel without wings. It was the girl selling flowers at the corner; her beauty went far beyond the tattered clothing she was wearing. The wealthy girls passing by giggled at her appearance. They were most definitely filled with jealousy at her natural beauty. Carlos crossed the street in a trance. His friends followed him, joking, but he could care less. Carlos stood in front of Carmelita and gently took the flowers from her hands; he then paid for them and turned around and handed them back to her. He said in a nervous voice, "These are for you." They looked at each other intensely and smiled. Carmelita then took the flowers and turned to the next costumer and sold them right in front of Carlos. He was so confused. Stuttering he said, "But ... but ... but they were for you?" Looking over her shoulders as she grabbed the money, Carmelita answered, "That's right, they are mine to do with as I please, right? And I please to sell them and make money." Carlos just stood there in disbelief. Carmelita then looked at him and said, "Are you going to buy more or just stand there and stare at me?" Carlos' best friend Armando noticed the defeat on his friend's face. Grabbing his friend's arm, he pulled him away. "All right, Romeo, so she's beautiful. But it's obvious you lost this battle. Let's go. You have made yourself enough of a fool for one day." Carmelita put one hand over her eyes to cover the sun and turned around to catch a glimpse of this handsome, tall stranger as he was being dragged away. Carlos too turned around to catch her smile.

Carlos went back every day to buy flowers from Carmelita. He even went as far as making a deal with her to make small flower arrangements for his mother daily. This was just an excuse for him to see her and talk to her. I mean, of course, he truly did want to make his mother happy too. Finally one day, Carlos asked her out for ice cream. To his surprise she accepted. This was Carmelita's first date ever. She was nervous but excited too. She put on her best dress and let her blonde, wavy hair down. Taking a long look into the mirror she sighed and said, "Here goes nothing. I hope you're ready for this!" Carmelita did not look her age; she was a mature young woman in body and mind.

After Carlos picked her up, they went for a stroll in the park. There they ate ice cream and chatted. But not much. It was very awkward, they were both very nervous. But Carlos broke the nervousness and began to ask a million questions. He wanted to know everything about Carmelita. All of her likes and dislikes, wants and needs. He just sat there in awe, listening to her talk. After a while his ice cream started to melt onto his hand and then onto his shirt cuff, making a mess. When she noticed, Carmelita got closer to him and began to clean him. He did not miss this opportunity, but he grasped a hold of it and stole a kiss from her lips. Carmelita was shocked but smiled, and her already rosy chicks turned even redder as she blushed. It was the sweetest moment either of them had experienced. And at that moment, up in heaven, an angel picked up his feathery pen and began writing the chronicles of our lives.

From that moment on, they were inseparable. They did not care about anyone or anything. Carlos was twenty years old, and for the first time in his life he was in love. There was no putting up an act, or keeping up appearances; it was all wonderfully transparent. Carmelita had just turned sixteen and was gorgeous. A simple and honest girl, she was a breath of fresh air to Carlos. Armando was their only friend. It seemed that everyone else did not agree with Carlos' choice for a girlfriend. Soon Sofia found out about her son's new love interest from the women who gossiped in town. It seemed as if Victoria, who belonged to one of the richest families in Mexico City, wanted Carlos for herself. Sofia and Victoria had already planned to trap Carlos into a summer wedding, but they were too late. His heart already belonged to another, and he was going to pay a high price for this precious love. A very high price. Carlos stayed up most of the night praying for wisdom. He knew he needed it with his mother. The next morning, armed with his love, prayers, and a stomach full of butterflies, he started a conversation with his mother. Kissing Sofia on the forehead he said, "Good morning, Mother, I have something to tell you. For me it is the best thing that has ever happened. Other than being your son, that is." Sofia knew what this was leading to, so quickly she interrupted him and reminded him of the dinner party she had planned for him and Victoria. She made sure to point out to him to be on time and be sure not to forget to buy the engagement ring today. She told him that everyone who was somebody would be coming. As she continued on and on, Carlos stopped her, "Mama, aren't you listening? I have something to tell you and it's important to me. And no! I'm not going to ask Victoria to marry me. I already asked someone else!" Sofia turned around and as she hit the table with her hand she said, "You are not going to marry that peasant girl! I did not struggle so you can marry someone below you! You will get the engagement ring today, and tomorrow night at dinner you will ask for Victoria's hand in marriage! You will marry Victoria, and that's final!" Carlos looked at his mother with great sadness on his face and in his voice. He said, "I have never disobeyed you, but today you give me no choice." He walked out of the room, knowing that all was lost between them. Sofia called for her driver and left the house to go about her business. She was sure that he would come around and obey her. He always had before.

Not aware of the situation, Carmelita got up early in the morning and began her day. First she went to get fresh flowers at the vendors, and then came back to make her arrangements. By eleven she made her way to the university corner where she sold her flowers daily. As she was busy making her arrangements on a table beside her cart, singing songs to the birds that hung in a cage from her flower cart, she felt someone staring at her. She turned around to say a happy good morning, but was faced with Sofia, who had a stern, hard look on her face. There Sofia stood in all her glory, checking Carmelita up and down. She began to walk around Carmelita and with a sarcastic tone of voice said, "So this is what my son is wasting his time with? This barbarian, dirty little girl, and gold digger. How much are you going to cost me? Five hundred pesos or maybe six hundred?" By this time, Carmelita put two and two together and knew that this had to be Carlos' mother. She was shaking from top to bottom but managed to say, in a humble tone of voice, "Señora, I love your son Carlos very much. I might not have any money like you, but I will gladly give my life for your son. That's how much I love him. My heart is rich in love for Carlos, Señora, and you can't put a price on that." By a miracle of God, Carlos walked into the conversation and put his arm around Carmelita, saying, "Well, Mother, I see that you have met the woman I love, but not properly. Please allow me to reintroduce you to each other. Carmelita, this is my mother, Sofia. Mom, this is the love of my life, Carmelita." Sofia dismissed his statement and arrogantly said, "If you want to play with this trashy, cheap little doll, you go right ahead. But don't make the mistake of thinking this will turn into something bigger and better or go any further. You understand? Don't you dare!" Carlos looked shocked and responded, "Mother, why can't I marry the women I love? Is it because she is poor? I'll make her rich. Or are you, Señora Sofia, worried about what people will say? Maybe it is because you didn't handpick her for me?" Sofia slapped Carlos as he continued. "Is that why you don't approve of her? Because, for the first time in my life, I made a decision without first consulting you? Go on, Mother, give me a good reason. I love her with all my heart. And unless you can tear my heart out of my chest, I'll always love her!" Sofia could not believe that her son was talking to her that way. She screamed back, "Stop being melodramatic, son. It doesn't become you. Get a hold of yourself; she's nothing but a gold digger. You think she loves you, but she doesn't love you; she loves what you are and the money you have. Without money, this love affair won't last. She'll tear you apart and leave you. I know her kind." She continued to say as she began to walk away, leaving, "Over my dead body will she ever be more then a dirty, wishful-thinking little tramp." Carlos said, on a last attempt to make her understand, "Mother, father has been gone for a long time and you still mourn him. I know you do. That's the kind of love I feel for her. It will never die." Sofia turned and pointing her finger at his face, visibly upset, and told him, "Don't you even compare this to the love your father and I once had. You have but only one day to make up your mind. Either you get the engagement ring for Victoria, or you can forget about the only life you have ever known! And me. If you pursue this ridiculous relationship, Carlos, I'll be forced to disown you. It's your choice." She walked away as Carmelita followed her. "Señora! You don't mean that, do you? This is your son. Your only child. He loves me, Señora. And I him. Please! I promise to love him and respect him. I'll make you proud. I'll work day and night to make more money!" Sofia, ignoring her, kept walking. "Please, Señora! Don't make him choose between you and me." Sofia pushed her out of her way and got into her limousine. She drove off, leaving them both standing there. Carmelita was in tears and Carlos speechless. They kept their eyes fixed on the back window, hoping she would look back and stop the car, but she never did.

Carlos and Carmelita embraced each other. Their hearts were heavy with sadness. Carmelita said to Carlos, "My love, I don't want you to lose your mother for me. I never knew mine and it is the saddest feeling in the world. A feeling like no other. I don't want to be responsible for you losing yours. You'll hate me in the end." She kissed him on the cheek and turned around and grabbed her cart and began to push it. Carlos stood there speechless for a minute or two, gathering his thoughts. Then, grabbing her by the arm, he told her, "Carmelita, go pack your bags. I'll be back in about two hours to take you to the courthouse to be my wife. Then we are going to go away. As soon as we're back from our honeymoon, we will have a small wedding at the church. Now, go and get your aunties; I'll get my friend Armando to meet us there to be my witness." Placing one hand over her mouth he continued, "Not a word, Carmelita. We're getting married. I'm not about to lose you, for nothing and no one. Mother is unreasonable sometimes. Putting fear in people's hearts is what she's best at, but she'll come around after we wed. I'm her only child." Removing her hands from the cart, he pushed it back in the storage room and locked the door. He said, "My wife doesn't sell flowers anymore." After giving her a hug he walked away. When he got to his car, she was still standing there in a daze. He turned and yelled back, "Two hours, my love! Be ready!" He got in the car and drove off. Carmelita stood there for a minute or two, thinking, and then she ran to her house and, filled with excitement, told her aunties, "I'm getting married to Carlos today! In two hours! Help me!" They immediately hugged and congratulated her and began to get her ready. Carmelita took out the very same dress she wore on their first date. Softly kissing it, she said to herself, "This is my lucky dress. I will wear it for my wedding." Auntie Lola got busy and made her a beautiful flower arrangement for her hands, and Anita a crown of daisies for her head.

Carlos went straight to the bank and took all of his money out and closed all his accounts. They were surprised at the bank but could not stop him. He then also emptied his deposit boxes, where he had all his bonds, stocks, jewelry, and personal papers. After that he drove straight to his house, where he called the trustworthy servants and asked them to help him pack. Quickly, he gave them instructions on what to pack and what to leave behind. Nobody minded helping him; he was loved by all. He asked José the gardener to keep an eye out for Sofia's car, but she never showed up. Finishing and looking around with great sadness, he said his goodbyes, first to his old nannies, and then to all the others. "I love you all," he said, and waved goodbye.

Two hours later, just as he promised, Carlos was back at the spot and he picked everyone up. Armando met them at the courthouse. Because Carmelita was under age, her aunties signed the papers giving her away. Armando was Carlos' witness. Hugs were exchanged with good wishes, and away they went. They made a quick stop to one of the small banks in town, where he deposited most of his money in both of their names and also opened a safe box. They then set off on their honeymoon to a grand hotel in Acapulco, which Carlos had quickly arranged. As they drove off to what was supposed to be the greatest moment in their life, Carlos had a heavy sadness inside. This was without a doubt the happiest moment of his life, but it was tainted by the unexplainable hatred Sofia had for Carmelita. It wasn't easy for him to go against her will, but he had no other choice. It was at this point that in heaven the second chapter in the book of our lives began.

A few days passed and Sofia was going out of her mind because she was so angry, worried, and upset about what had happened. She had driven to Carmelita's house on many occasions but never stopped. She was too proud. Her pride was hurt beyond repair when Carlos disobeyed her. To her this was unforgivable. She swore revenge on Carmelita, and she was definitely someone to be afraid of. She had questioned Armando intensely, but he did not give in to her. In the meantime, Carlos and Carmelita got back from their honeymoon and had their small church wedding. The priest knew the circumstances and had previously agreed to marry them when they came back. The wedding was simple but filled with love, good wishes, and blessings. Carmelita wore a white satin wedding dress with a big ribbon on the back. She looked beautiful. To adorn her blondish hair she wore a crown of fresh roses and a veil that covered her face and went down to her feet. In her hands she had a bouquet of red roses too. She once again was an angel without wings. Carlos was very handsome and wore his black and white tuxedo, with his best man Armando by his side. He could not be any happier this day.

Except for his mother's absence, it would have been a perfect day. The church was filled with flowers and friends, all of whom had best wishes for them. The ceremony was short and lovely, and, of course, Maria and her family came too. After the wedding, everyone was invited to the reception, which took place in the courtyard of Carlos and Carmelite's new apartment. Carmelita's aunties had cooked up storm the night before, preparing loads of food. It was a beautiful party celebrating the two young lovers' vows for each other. Everyone feasted and danced until the early hours of the morning.

Their new apartment was very modest in comparison to what Carlos was accustomed to, but it was their love nest and he could not be any happier. For Carmelita, it was amazing to be married to Carlos and have their own home, which they would fill with memories. The only thing in her life that was missing still was her family. This constantly tore her inside. One afternoon while Carlos was at work, she decided to invite Maria for coffee. Carmelita asked Maria about her past. Maria, realizing she was entitled to the truth, told her everything. There were moments of anger, tears, and silence, but she got to know every detail of her life. From that moment on, Carmelita begin to pray for her father, and asked God that maybe someday their paths would cross. She promised herself that her firstborn would be named after her father Angelo in his honor.

Carlos never went back to the university. Instead he got an excellent job as a junior editor with a publication company called Arte & Cultura (Art & Culture). Carmelita became a homemaker and went back to school. She wanted to educate herself and make her husband proud. Armando used to come and visit them, bringing news from home. "Everyone knows you got married," he told Carlos. "There is gossip and talk all over, and your mom has gotten worse, if you know what I mean. Everyone fears her, now more than ever." Putting his hand on Carlos' shoulder, he said, concerned, "My friend, be careful. I'm afraid the worst is yet to come."

A neighbor, who was a professional tailor and lived in the same apartment complex as Carlos and Carmelita, had befriended Carmelita. Esther was her name. She was a nice lady with no kids of her own. She took a liking to this young newlywed girl, and she began to teach Carmelita everything she knew about making suits and dresses. Carmelita was a quick learner and she picked it up very fast. Together they began to work and make good money. Carmelita, wanting to have a big family, dreamed of a house that she could fill with children. She saved her money carefully, and when she thought she had enough she surprised Carlos with it. Between the two of them, they now had enough money for a down payment on a house. They found an adorable three-bedroom house with a side garage that they converted into a small tailor shop for Carmelita. Life was good to them. If only Sofia could be a part of it. Carlos missed his mother so much. But he was cut off from her and he understood this would not change unless he left Carmelita. That was out of the question.

Sofia had plunged herself into her work, trying to forget her only son. Her so-called friends constantly made hurtful remarks to her. Yet these things never fazed her. She tried to go on with her life, sometimes asking herself what she was living for. She had nobody, but she was never going to give in to Carmelita. Sofia's hate and stubbornness had overtaken her life.

Carmelita and Carlos were very happy together and worked hard for their dreams to come true. When they had their first child, they named him Angelo in honor of her dad, just like she said she would. Then she promised Carlos that the next baby boy would be named after him. As for Carlos, he did not care. He knew he was blessed with Carmelita and Angelo. It was his beautiful family of three. After the birth of his son, Carlos decided to write Sofia a letter. In it he included a picture of Angelo.

Dearest Mom,

I have missed you so much. But since I know how stubborn you can be, I kept my distance. I'm the happiest man in this world. I hope someday you can be happy for my wife and me too. The baby in this photo is your first grandchild. He has your eyes and your stubbornness too. Carmelita has her own tailoring business. It is small but very successful. I, on the other hand work as a Junior Editor, but I'm sure you already know that. We miss you, Mom, and you're very welcome in our humble home any time. I'm proud of the life I have created for my family and the man I have become. I am not ashamed for not having as much as you. There is love in my home and there is love for Grandma too. If you someday find it in your heart to contact me, I would very much so appreciate it and look forward to having you back in my life. I pray for you each and every day and hope that God has blessed you and continues to take care of you.

Love,

Your Son Carlos, Carmelita, and baby Angelo.

With that Carlos sent the letter, which he had hand-delivered. He thought maybe now with a grandson she'd change her mind. And maybe, just maybe, all of that hatred that she had felt for so long would melt away now that she knew that there's a baby involved. Sofia received it that same day. She closed her office door and told her secretary not disturb her. As she sat down to read it, many thoughts ran through her mind. She thought that maybe they needed money, or that her son was sick, or better yet, maybe she wanted to come home. As she opened the letter, the baby's picture fell down on her lap. She froze for a minute, and then she went on to read the letter. Picking up the baby's picture, she kissed it. She had a grandchild. She stared at the baby's picture and found her beloved Carlo. The baby looked just like he had. It looked just like Carlo and, of course, her Carlitos as well. Even as she tried to bury the past it had caught up with her. She bitterly cried and held the picture close to her heart. She began to daydream about when Carlo was alive, the love, the plans, and the dreams. Suddenly there was a knock on her door, which brought her back out of her daydream. She yelled, "I told you not to disturb me!" As the door opened up, there was Carlos, Carmelita, and baby Angelo. Baby Angelo had a big smile on his face and pointed at Sofia. Sofia stood up and reached for the baby. She kissed him and hugged him as she held him close to her chest. She told him, "I love you, my precious one, just as I love my son." She motioned for them to sit down and was still holding Angelo when she said to Carlos, "Come here and give your mother a kiss." Then she went on to say, "I read your letter and I want you to immediately come back home and work here. Come and run the companies I have created. It is time for you to take your place in the family. I will retire and watch over my grandson." Then she looked over to Carmelita and, looking away, she continued, "You have managed to change everyone's life for a long time. It is time for me to change yours. First, I want to baptize the baby. Then I'll put together a big party to properly introduce him to society. We also need to hire a tutor for you, to teach you proper manners. In regards to your house, you may give it to her aunts so they can leave that hell-hole they live in. To them it will be a palace. I will not allow my grandson to grow up away from me another second." Calling her assistant, she gave her orders to cancel all appointments for that week. "Better yet make it the in entire month," she said. "Today we're going shopping for everyone. And then you are all going to move in. I have not been this excited in a long time," she murmured, kissing Angelo's forehead. She opened her office door and began to give orders to everyone as they walked past them. Carlos and Carmelita were astonished; they had prayed and hoped for a change in her heart, but this was more than they had ever expected.

They moved into Sofia's house that afternoon. Coming in they got a wonderful, warm welcome from all the staff. They were a breath of fresh air in that house. There were people running every which way. Nannies were lined up for interviews, as were baby furniture designers and consultants. It was a mad house. For Carmelita it was all foreign; she was lost. Once they settled in, they were a little saddened to have to let go of everything they had worked so hard for. It was as if their arm of independence was cut off, and Sofia made sure of it.

A year passed by and it went great. Everything was working out. Carmelita was educated in all levels, and Carlos was running everything. It was doing even better than when Sofia was in charge. People worked for him happily, not because of fear as when they worked with Sofia. Sofia managed to get along with Carmelita, and baby Angelo was getting bigger and growing up. Everything seemed perfect. It was too perfect. Sofia's conniving ways were getting the best of her. Sofia plotted behind their backs constantly. She sent woman after woman to tempt Carlos, but they all failed because Carlos' heart belonged to only one woman. She also made her friends' daughters befriend Carmelita so that they could spy on her. But Carmelita's kindness and warm heart won them over time after time. They all ended up telling on Sofia, but Carmelita always made excuses for her. She wanted her so badly to love her like a daughter, and Carmelita actually believed that she did. Sofia continued to fail and became frustrated. This was dangerous because it would make her take more daring risks to separate them. One morning Sofia heard them laughing and giggling in the library. When she heard the commotion, she came in and asked, "What is all this noise I hear?" Carlos proudly announced, "Mother, Carmelita is expecting!" Carmelita told Sofia, "Maybe this time I'll have a little girl, and I would be honored if you allowed me to name her Sofia." Carlos jokingly said, "No, no. This time it is Carlitos Jr. Remember?" Sofia felt faint. She was so surprised and clearly upset that she had to sit down. Carlos, looking at her reaction, was puzzled. He asked her, "What is wrong, Mother?" She lied, saying, "I'm just so happily surprised." But only her dark heart knew her real thoughts. And happy she was not.

Sofia began plotting against Carmelita's pregnancy right away. Even the staff noticed her intense dislike for Carmelita and felt sorry for her. Many times they even kept her away from Sofia in order to keep her safe. But one morning, as Carmelita had morning sickness, she made the mistake of asking Sofia what she could do for the sickness. Sofia told her to go to the medicine cabinet and look for a prescription by the name of Promosio. "You need to take four pills and lay down." She then turned her back to Carmelita and smiled deceivingly, whispering to herself, "You'll get rid of your sickness all right and much more." Carmelita followed her instructions exactly; after all, Sofia loved baby Angelo. Why would she hurt an unborn child? Little did she know the medicine she was taking was considered poison to someone with child.

Carlos became very busy as he took over all the businesses; he was constantly working odd hours and was away from home most of the time. This particular day he became homesick and wanted to be with his family, so he decided to cancel all appointments and meetings and go home to spend some quality time with his son and young wife. When he came home he found Carmelita at the top of the stairs, holding her stomach. She said, "Carlos, I feel sick." Carlos ran up the stairs just in time to catch her as she fainted. He yelled to the servants to call the doctor and carried her to their bedroom. By the time he laid her on the bed, his hands and suit were saturated with blood. Carmelita had already begun to miscarry. In desperation, Carlos tried to wake her up. Yelling for Sofia, he pleaded with God. Sofia walked in, trying to wipe her smile from her face. "What's wrong son?" she said, acting shocked. Carlos told her how he had found Carmelita. Being the great actress she was, Sofia managed to look concerned and tried to help out. She knew it was too late to save the child. She had already succeeded in her evil scheme. The baby was dead. Carmelita, however, lived. Although she knew the truth, she never told Carlos what really happened. She feared he would want to leave immediately. Carmelita freely became Sofia's victim, just so Carlos would have his mother's love and her son a real grandma, even if the source of the love came from an evil person like Sofia.

One day late in December that year, it was raining and the stairs were slippery. Sofia told the servants not to wipe them dry as they usually did. Instead she sent for Carmelita and asked her to go downstairs to get her the book that she had laid down in the study room on top of the piano. She claimed that no one else would be able to find it. She told Carmelita to leave Angelo with her. Putting the baby on the bed beside Sofia, Carmelita went down to get her the book. As she went down the stairway she slipped and fell down all the way to the bottom of the stairs. When Sofia heard the screams, she turned to Angelo in her evil tone and said, "I hope your mommy broke her neck!" Immediately the ambulance was called, and Carmelita was rushed to the hospital. In front of Carlos, Sofia acted unbelievably upset at all the servants. She fired half of the staff for not drying the stairs. They were all so terrified of the repercussions if they told Carlos the truth that they just left without a word. Thank God Carmelita had only broken one leg and some ribs. Although she was banged up very badly, she was still alive. When the news reached Sofia, it was too much for her. She basically went off the deep end, and her madness worsened as she whispered to herself, "That snake won't die."

Suspecting foul play, Carlos asked Carmelita, "What happened? What really happened?" She simply said, "It was an accident. It was wet and I slipped and fell." Carlos only believed her because he knew that Carmelita would not lie to him. But something inside told him that things just weren't right. He began to feel that too many mishaps were occurring. And it seemed that they were only happening to Carmelita when he wasn't home. Then he remembered his friend Armando's words: "I fear the worst is yet to come." Carmelita's recovery was a slow and painful one. She was bedridden, yet Sofia could not be any happier. She talked the doctors into making her stay in the hospital and away from home for as long as they could. Sofia used this time to get closer to her son, getting on his good side. She went out of her way to be the most wonderful mother and grandma that she possibly could be.

It was clear this was a no-win situation for Sofia. She could not get rid of Carmelita on her own. So she carefully began to ask around how much it would cost for someone to make an accident happen. A deadly accident. As word got around in dark corners and bars, someone finally answered her inquiry. A small, fat, and dark man by the name of Sanchez contacted Sofia. He had no problem doing the hit, but he had to get permission from someone before it could be done. He told Sofia he would contact her in a couple of days. Sanchez left Mexico City and went to Cuernavaca to get the blessing for the hit from Don Juan Carlos de La Peña. De La Peña was the Mexican Godfather, who immediately after listening to Mr. Sanchez refused the hit and ordered Sanchez not to execute it. His last words to Sanchez were, "If anything happens to her or anyone in that family, I will personally deal with that animal myself." And with that he gestured to Sanchez to leave. Sanchez was confused; there was a lot of money involved, but he dared not question the boss.

That night, smoking a Cuban cigar, overlooking the city below, Juan Carlos de La Peña struggled with the decision that he had to make. *I'm an old man,* he thought. *I don't have much time left, and that young innocent couple needs to know what is going on.* He wrestled all night with what to do. He knew it was getting too dangerous for Carmelita, and even for Carlos and the baby. It was obvious that if Sofia was looking for an assassin she was out of control. Having known and dealt with Sofia in the past, he knew that she was a very vicious woman. Although he had made excuses for her behavior previously, this was too much even for him. You see, Don Juan Carlos de La Peña had moved to Cuernavaca shortly after Carlitos turned two. He had moved there to keep and eye on his nephew and to protect Sofia and make her wealthy. Don Juan Carlos de La Peña, after all, was aka Giovanni. He sat in his brown leather chair in front of the fireplace and reminisced about his youth, when his brother Carlo and he first came to Monterrey, Mexico. Young and scared, memories flashed in his head. He said, talking to his dead brother, "I swore over your dead body that I would look after Sofia and your son. And I have not let you down. Talk to me, brother; tell me how to handle this." He took a sip of his drink and put his head down between his hands as if waiting for an answer to fall down from heaven. For so many years he had known exactly what to do in every situation, but this was so different, this was family. Giovanni was a prominent doctor by day and respected by everyone. By night he was a powerful Godfather. He was even more powerful then the president of the Mexico himself. Giovanni, he had never married and stayed alone, building a stronghold for Sofia and his only true link to his bloodline, his nephew Carlos. His mission in life had been to protect them. That's what he lived for. And now his nephew Carlos needed his protection for his loving wife Carmelita.

Chapter V

As the morning approached, still sitting in his brown leather chair, Giovanni saw the sun come up. He knew in his heart what had to be done, but he also knew it would ultimately put everyone in danger. He had powerful enemies himself, but none as bad as Sofia was to Carmelita and ultimately Carlos. Giovanni got up and told all of his men to get ready; they were going to the airport. His right-hand man, Leonardo, asked, "Boss, where are we going?" "To Mexico City to see...," and then he paused. "To see friends of mine." As soon as they arrived in Mexico City, he planned to go straight to see Carlos. It was essential. They needed to talk man to man. After that, they both could talk to Carmelita. He would then go to the house to see Sofia. As the drove off, he was planning what to say. Admittedly he was anxious over what he had to do, but he was also excited about possibly finally reconciling with his family. Even if it had to be over something as terrible as Sofia's madness, which had taken her over. As the car turned the corner, two police cars blocking the street stopped them. One of the officers approached the car by himself. Juan Carlos whispered to everyone to stay calm.

"Do not make a move." As he rolled down the window, he said, "Good morning, Officer. What seems to be the problem?" Looking at his ID, he caught his name. "Officer Ochoa? Why are we being stopped?" Ochoa leaned in the window and answered, "Well, well. If it isn't Mr. Juan Carlos de La Peña. You know, there are rumors about you. We would like to check them out. But first, are your boys armed?" Cool, calm, and collected Juan Carlos asked, "Why? Is there a war happening that we don't know about?" The officer replied, "Well, why is a prominent doctor like you being protected so heavily? Are you afraid someone is not happy with their new prescriptions?" With a grin on his face and a calm voice, Juan Carlos answered, "Here's a little something for your family." Leonardo handed him 2,000 pesos all folded up. "Have a great day and stop wasting mine." The officer pushed the money aside. "I'm afraid this is not going to be that easy. We need you to follow us to the police station. There is a car behind you already and we will escort you in the front. Please, Señor, follow us." With that, Ochoa walked away and got in the police car in front. To say the least, Juan Carlos was very upset, but he kept his cool. He had people on the inside.

Once at the police station, the chief of police realized what his detective had done and came down running and apologizing to Juan Carlos. You see, the chief was on de La Peña's payroll. He was absolutely sorry and was going to take care of that insolent Ochoa immediately. How dare he put Don Juan Carlos through something like this? The chief personally walked everyone out and made sure they were not offended. He knew dealing with Juan Carlos de La Peña that his neck was on the line. Literally. After listening to his constant apologizing, Juan Carlos told the chief of police to relax and get out of his face. They needed to leave. Juan Carlos was running out of patience and told Leonardo to hire more men; he did not need these kinds of delays ever again. And regarding the chief he said, "That imbecile is nothing but a waste of skin. But he has a family; leave him be." They then went to a restaurant where he was already set to meet Orasio.

When they got to the restaurant, Orasio was already waiting for them outside, looking like a scared mouse and walking around his car talking to himself. Juan Carlos was dropped in front of the restaurant with Leonardo and the others. One of Juan Carlos' men told Orasio to go in and talk to Juan Carlos. When he entered, he was shaking from top to bottom. He said, "Mr. De La Peña, I know where Don Carlos is today. He's at the factory. Piedras Blanca. He should be getting out of a meeting any time now." Juan Carlos asked what mood is he in. Orasio answered, "Don Carlos? He's always pleasant and kind. He's the best." Without hesitating Juan Carlos said, "All right. Let's go!" Automatically everyone dropped their food and followed him to the cars.

They drove straight to the plant and he told everyone to wait outside. Juan Carlos went in alone except for Leonardo, who followed him inside but also stayed far enough behind to keep an eye on things. Giovanni thought, *I'm here to meet my nephew at last.* As he smiled, he walked through the reception area and got in the elevator with a girl running after him, asking if she could help. Quickly Leonardo took care of her. He got off on the third floor and was greeted by a secretary by the name of Ofelia, who promptly got up, asking, "Can I help you? Do you have an appointment?" He said, "I'm here to see my nephew Carlos." Ofelia did not find this amusing, saying, "What is this? A joke? My boss has no family but Dona Sofia, his wife, and baby Angelo. Who are you?" Carlos heard the commotion outside his door. Opening it he asked Ofelia, "What in the world is going on?" Visibly upset she answered, "This man claims to be your uncle, Señor." Carlos walked through his door saying, "Mr....," waiting for a name. "I'm sure your nephew is somewhere, but not here and I'm not him. I have no uncles. No family at all." Giovanni stood there, staring at Carlos. "You look just like my brother Carlo, your father." Knowing his father's name shocked Carlos. How in the world can this total stranger know his father's name? He asked, "How do you know that?" Giovanni gestured, "We should go into your office and talk, my nephew." As they walked in, Giovanni began to tell him about his father and the circumstances that had led to the present. Giovanni gave him a hug and, kissing him on both cheeks, said in Italian, "At last, at last." He continued to tell him the rest of the story. "I'm known as Doctor Juan Carlos de La Peña. I had to start a new life, just like Sofia did for your safety." Giovanni took his hat off and sat down, gesturing for Carlos to do the same. He continued, saying again in amazement, "You look just like your father." He pulled an old picture from his wallet and pointed at Carlo and Sofia at their wedding. "This was my big brother, your father. I am Giovanni, his little brother from Sicily," he said, reintroducing himself. He went on to tell him how Sofia and Carlo met and fell in love, and how much they loved each other. "Wait! Wait!" Carlos said, stunned.

"You mean to tell me all this time I had you, a living relative?" Giovanni said, "My dear nephew, Sofia was trying to protect you. You see, your father was assassinated. Please understand, Nephew." And calming him down, he continued to tell him the rest. Two hours passed by and Ofelia was getting worried. Slowly she opened the door as she knocked softly. She asked, "Señor Carlos, do you need anything?" Carlos answered, "Please, Ofelia, cancel everything for the day. Don't interrupt us anymore. And send for Chinese food. You do like Chinese, don't you, Uncle?" he asked Giovanni. To that he answered, "I love Chinese!" Carlos said, "Please go on, Uncle. I want to know everything!" walking around his desk to take a seat again. When Giovanni got to the part of why they left Sicily, he told Carlos, "Nephew, this is about honor, misunderstanding, and position. It is time I tell someone. Your own mother doesn't even know this story."

Before he could begin, they were interrupted when Ofelia knocked on the door to tell Carlos that his wife was on the phone. "I'll take it," answered Carlos. He picked up the phone and excitedly said, "Carmelita, what are you doing, my love?" She replied, "Laying here with my leg up in the air, wishing I was there," and she laughed. "How would you like for me to come right now and bring you Chinese food?" Even though she was dying to see her husband, Carmelita knew what a busy man he was. She said, "My dearest, don't worry yourself about me. I was just calling because I'm bored. Please forgive me and go back to work." So excited about wanting to share everything he'd just learned with his wife, Carlos said, "No, no. We're coming over right now. There is someone I want you to meet today. We'll be there soon." With that he hung up. Picking up his hat he said, "Let's go, Uncle. Let's go meet my wife! I know there's more for me to find out, but you have to meet my wife. You'll love her! She is the sweetest, kindest person you'll ever meet!" Smiling, Giovanni said, "I love her already, Nephew. She is indeed an extraordinary young woman." As they got in the elevator, Carlos made a very important comment, stating, "I'm a very lucky guy. Carmelita puts up with Mom, and it is not easy." His uncle looked at him, saying, "I wish you had known your mother the way I did, before she became what she is now. She was sweet, full of life, and a kind, young, beautiful girl. But when she lost your father, she lost herself too. Nephew, be very careful with your wife. Keep an eye on her. Good women are hard to find." Carlos couldn't help but notice two cars were following them as they drove off. Suspicious, he said, "Uncle Giovanni, I think we're are being followed." Giovanni kind of chuckled, saying, "It is just my people. Don't worry, Nephew, you'll get used to them."

They got to the hospital, and Carlos presented his uncle to Carmelita. Giovanni, being the gentleman he was, took his hat off and kissed her hand. "You are as beautiful as I imagined, my dear." Carmelita blushed and smiled. "You are too kind, Señor, but what is going on?" she asked. "My love, I have an uncle and much more! But don't worry. We will explain everything later on." Carmelita was ecstatic for her husband. She just stared at both of them standing in front of her. "Now I see where you got your good looks," she said. Laughing, Giovanni said, "I like this girl."

Later Giovanni and Carlos went on to try to explain everything to Carmelita. Of course, they sugarcoated most of it. Carmelita was so excited, she said to Carlos, "You're Sicilian too!" She then went on to tell Uncle Giovanni what she knew about her parents. "Hmm. Perhaps I can help you locate your family. But for now we need to let you rest." Begging she said, "Please don't go! I want to go home. I can be in bed at home too!" Giovanni looked at Carlos, saying, "She's got a point, you know." With that, they spoke to the doctor and he released her. They put Carmelita in an ambulance and followed her home.

As the ambulance pulled into the circular drive at Sofia's house, Sofia was furious. She knew it had to be Carmelita coming home. Suddenly she saw Carlos' car pull up behind it, but she could not make out who was with him. She took a deep breath and fixed her dress and went to the door as she faked a smile and display of happiness that Carmelita came home. The first thing Carmelita asked for was Angelo. In the meantime, as Carlos and Giovanni got out of the car, Giovanni said to him, "I don't know what to expect from Sofia. But what ever happens in there, know that I have always loved you and protected both of you with my life." Carlos put his arm around him and said, "Welcome home, Uncle. Welcome home."

They walked in through the double front doors, and Sofia took a long look at this stranger, trying to recognize the wrinkled face. She then walked a few steps closer to him and realized that Giovanni stood before her. "What are you doing here, Giovanni?" she exclaimed. "Why are you here? Are you out of your mind? Why have you brought your curse to my family?" Giovanni expected nothing less from Sofia. He knew what a mean old woman she had become, but under all of that he was hoping that something good had survived over the years. If indeed it had, he hoped it would surface now. Giovanni asked, "Sofia, may I have a seat?" She gestured for him to sit. "Look at you, Sofia. You look fantastic! You are still as beautiful as I remember." Sofia interrupted him. "You think that by all of your chivalries I'm going to forgive you for keeping me in the dark all of those years. I was just a young girl, Giovanni! I needed to know." Giovanni looked down, saddened. "I know, Sofi, but it is too late for what we should have done, or could have done. The past is gone. Let's talk about the future." Still standing and pacing back and forth, Sofia exclaimed, "What future? We don't have a future." Giovanni replied, "Indeed we do. Dearest Carlos and Carmelita know everything. You cannot erase me anymore." Sofia was about to unload when Carlos put his arm around her and said, "All right, it has being a full, wonderful day for all of us. I'm sure that Uncle Giovanni needs to rest from his trip. Let me show you to your room, Uncle." Giovanni looked in Sofia's direction and said, "I'm not staying here where I'm not wanted. Sofia has to invite me to stay. It is only customary for the hostess to invite her guests. After all, this is her house." Looking at him in disapproval, Sofia said, "You can stay. But like you said and keep in mind, this is my house, Giovanni. My house. And keep your gorillas out of sight in the guest house." She then stomped out of the room. She was shaken up. Her world had collapsed in front of her, just like it had those years ago. Now there were two intruders in her house. Giovanni and Carmelita. It would be harder to get rid of two rats without suspicions arising.

As she walked through the house to her room she said to herself, "Sanchez will call me tomorrow. Maybe he will come up with the perfect solution for both of them." Giovanni went upstairs to his room. Knowing Sofia like he did, he called Sanchez and instructed him to contact her as previously arranged. "Let's see what the old witch has in mind," he told him.

The next morning they all met at the breakfast table. Giovanni got to play with baby Angelo and they all talked and laughed. It was if they were a family that had known each other for years. Well, except for Sofia, that is. She did not come down until later. When she did, she sat at the head of the table. This family reunion brought back a lot of painful memories for her. She imagined how things would have been had she not lost her husband and entire family all those years ago. She thought about her life had she not had to flee. But she kept strong, saying to Giovanni, "What is it that you want from us? Money? How much for you to disappear and never to come back?" Giovanni looked at Sofia and shook his head. "Sofia my dearest, I can't believe that you think of me like that. I have more money then the three of you put together. I'm a doctor and a very good one at that. You see, I have hidden under another name for years. I work under the name of Dr. Juan Carlos de La Peña. I will let you guys, my family, in on a highly guarded secret. You see, I also run other businesses, Sofi. I am what they call the 'Godfather' of Mexico."

Sofia, getting up, slammed her hand on the table. "You're what?" Sofia was beside herself with anger. Pointing at the door, she ordered Giovanni, "Get out! Get out of my house now!" Carlos got up from the table and got in between them. He said, "Mother, stop it. Please continue, Uncle." Sofia began to walk around the room pacing, but she kept her eyes on Giovanni the whole time. If looks could kill, he would have been dead. She was outraged. "How dare you bring this filth into my house, Giovanni. You're endangering all of us." Carlos gestured for Sofia to calm down. "Tell me, Uncle, baby Angelo is not in any kind of danger is he?" Giovanni leaned over to Carlos' ear and whispered, "As a matter of fact, he could not be better protected now that I'm here." Sofia, not knowing what Giovanni had just told Carlos, walked out of the room enraged.

Carlos asked Carmelita very politely to leave the room, and she rolled her wheelchair to Giovanni and took the baby from his arms. "Excuse us, Uncle," she said softly, "I know he's too young to understand, but he will get in the way," and she left the room. Carlos invited Giovanni to the study, where they poured themselves a drink, lit up a cigar, and sat across from each other. Giovanni began to talk about Carlo. Carlos asked, "Was he also a Mafioso?" Giovanni answered quickly saying, "No! My brother hated that kind of life. It is actually what killed him." He went on to tell Carlos about when the two were growing up in Sicily. He continued to explain to Carlos that his father, Carlo, was the oldest and the smartest, and when they got to Mexico he went through a lot to keep them both safe and to make a good life for them both. Carlos asked him, "What took you so long to come and look for me, Uncle?" Giovanni thought for a minute. "I guess I felt it was necessary to stay away. You needed to grow up, and I knew that Sofia was still upset at me. But now you see it is necessary for me to be here."

While the men were talking, Carmelita took baby Angelo into the courtyard to play. Sofia knew that she had to move faster than she had planned. She could not wait for Sanchez to call her back. She also was afraid that Giovanni would find out about the hit on Carmelita. Her thoughts were running crazy in her mind, when she heard Angelo laughing. She turned toward the courtyard and saw Carmelita and baby Angelo playing. Carmelita's leg was still in a cast and she sat in the wheelchair, doing her best to keep up with the quick and playful Angelo. Sofia hated Carmelita so badly and she wanted her dead. The sooner the better. At that point, Sofia came up with her next move. She walked in and said to Carmelita, "I thought that since you are feeling better that you can go with the driver to town to the pharmacy and pick up my prescription. I cannot make it there today. I am just not feeling well with all of this that is going on. Please, be a dear and go quickly." Sofia took Angelo from her arms, but Carmelita objected, saying, "I'd rather take Angelo with me. He would enjoy the mountain ride. It's a beautiful day after all." Sofia quickly answered, "No! No! Girl, just go. I feel faint-hearted." She convinced her to leave. Sofia quickly called for her groundskeeper, Ernesto. She instructed him to make a hole in the brake line of the Cadillac immediately. Ernesto asked, "Are you sure, Señora?" Sofia answered him in an ill manner. "Hurry up, you imbecile. There's no time to waste."

Carmelita grabbed her purse and a light sweater and was almost pushed out of the house by Sofia making sure that she would not have time to say goodbye to anyone. Before the car drove away, Carmelita looked back at Sofia and baby Angelo. It was almost as if she knew of Sofia's plan to kill her. Sofia walked into the study to keep everyone busy. Giovanni felt something was wrong. Sofia was too sweet all of a sudden. He asked where Carmelita was, but she did not answer him and continued with small talk, as if trying to evade the question. Having remembered hearing a car drive off, Giovanni then asked her again more directly. He got in front of Sofia and, grabbing her arms, he asked again, "Sofia! Where is Carmelita?" Sofia finally answered him, "I sent her for my medicine. Now let go of me!" Giovanni looked at her and said, "What have you done, woman?" and he left the room in a hurry.

He went to look for the others. He found Leonardo just outside the main entrance door. "Did you see her leave?" he asked. Leonardo said, "Yes, boss. Don't worry, boss. I stopped that idiot Ernesto." Giovanni asked, "What was he trying to do?" Leonardo smiled and said, "Let's just say that the brakes won't fail. And Ernesto is no longer in need of a job." Giovanni took a deep breath and said, "She's got to be stopped. I love her so, but she's got to be stopped." Leonardo nodded a yes with his head, looking down. Leonardo knew that Sofia was Giovanni's only connection to the past and to his brother. Giovanni went on to say, "Today around 5:00 in the afternoon, I will take Carlos and Carmelita into town for dinner with the baby. Sofia will be left alone. She's getting a new prescription, the one she sent Carmelita to get. Do we understand each other?" Leonardo said, "Yes, boss, completely." Still looking down out of respect, he knew this was hard for Giovanni. Very hard. Giovanni stood there for a couple of minutes. Thinking he had to break the promise he had guarded and kept for so long, this was the hardest decision he had ever had to make. But he knew it had to be done.

Sofia saw him talking to Leonardo through one of the big windows in the study. She intensely looked at Giovanni's face for a reaction. She began to ask herself if maybe he knew. She wondered what he was doing out there. She had all sorts of things going through her mind while Carlos was still talking to her. As Carlos noticed the lack of attention, he grabbed Sofia's arm and, turning her toward him, said, "For the last time, Mother, why is Uncle Giovanni so concerned about Carmelita?" She abruptly removed his hand from her arm and said, "What are you insinuating? That I would hurt her?" He took a step back and, speaking as if he was going out of his mind, he said, "All of this time ... all the accidents.... That's got to be it. That's why he said to me that he felt it was necessary to come into our lives. You just answered my question. It has been you who caused the accident and the miscarriage. I didn't want to believe it. You're my mother, my son's grandma. Why? Why! Don't you know she loves you so much? The poor girl always makes excuses for you. She has tried so hard to win your approval. Your love. But no! The Dona has forgotten to love anyone but herself!" Sofia was outraged as she yelled, "Enough with your insults! I love you! I make no excuses for my love for you. I have done everything for you and Angelo. I will continue to do everything in my power to get rid of that piece of trash you've forced me to take into our family!"

Carlos could not believe everything he was hearing. Giovanni walked back into the study and gestured with his hands for everyone to calm down. "Don't worry, Nephew, everything is under control," and he winked at Carlos. "Sofia, I have no words for you. My brother is crying in heaven for your soul. It's so full of hate and darkness, for what, huh? For whom? You have everything because I was always watching over you. Do you actually think that men would ever consider doing business with an inexperienced young woman? Of course not, but I was there to bend their wills. The marriage you arranged is about the only thing I've let you do on your own. But everything else, Sofia, all the success is because of me. I spoiled you, Sofi. I understand now. I caused you to think you're invincible. But you're not!" Sofia had to sit down. And for once she was speechless. Giovanni went on. "Everything that has happened in your life since Carlitos was a baby is my doing. I became who I am to make sure I could keep my promise to my brother Carlo. I provided protection and wealth for you both. Yes, I became the scam of the world for you both." He went on to say, "But you, Sofia, you have became a heartless monster. You have lost any and all of the goodness that once filled your heart. You're full of selfishness. You are increasingly becoming more dangerous, even to those that love you. You have to have respect for life, Sofi. You have no friends. No one. My dear sister-in-law, you leave me speechless. Do you understand that? You leave me speechless!"

Sofia got up from the chair and slowly walked toward Giovanni, and in an arrogant tone of voice said to him, "I guess now you'll decide our fate. I suppose Carmelita is going to live a long life and give me more grandchildren. And then we will live happily ever after. Or are you going to take my money away, huh? Should I be scared?" Giovanni felted mocked as she added, "So that we have a clear understanding of what could happen, your future is in my hands now, Giovanni. I know your secret and I can destroy you at will!" Exiting the study, she turned and said, looking straight at Giovanni, "I am going to lie down now, and don't bother saying goodbye. Just be sure that you leave my house."

Carlos was crushed. He could not believe what a monster his mother was. Giovanni put his hands on Carlos' shoulder, trying to bring him comfort, and said, "My dear nephew, I'm so sorry I had to open your eyes about your mother, but I could not stand by and let her keep going on like she has. One day she would succeed in her attempts to kill Carmelita." With his head down, Carlos said, "I know Mom is not an angel, but never did I imagine she was so sick with hate for Carmelita. I thought all of that was left behind us. Carmelita has suffered in silence for me to have my mother." Having figured everything out, a tear rolled down his cheek. "Uncle, our baby. She killed our baby. I'm sure of that. And Carmelita's accident, that had to be her doing too. Mother is sick. Very sick, and I was too blind to see it. I'm to be blamed too." Giovanni assured him nothing else would happen ever again. "Listen, Nephew, why don't we have dinner tonight, just the three of us and the baby? Let's go to town and we'll figure out our next move over dinner. It is time that we all have a little bit of fun instead of worrying about all of this."

Later that evening after Carmelita safely returned home, they all went to dinner. While Giovanni watched the baby, and although Carmelita still had a cast on, Carlos and Carmelita managed to dance to a slow, romantic song. It was one of the first times in a long time everyone had a good time. When they got home, Sofia was not up. They thought that she might have gone to bed early, so they kissed goodnight and went to bed. The next morning around eleven o'clock, one of the servant girls came and told Carmelita that Sofia was not up yet and that she was not responding to the knocking on her door either. Carmelita said, "I'll go see if I can get her." After attending to the baby she went to see about Sofia. Slowly opening the door, she said, "Mama Sofia, are you awake?" She noticed that the bed was untouched. She continue to go in, asking, "Mama Sofia, where are you?" Still there was no answer.

Carmelita continued into the room and she got to the bathroom, and there on the floor was the lifeless body of Sofia. Lying against the bathtub, her eyes were open and she had some sort of foam around her mouth. "Help! Someone call a doctor!" Carmelita yelled. Everyone came running. Carmelita was on the floor by Sofia's side, crying as she held her cold hand. Giovanni picked Carmelita up from the floor and sat her on the bed. Then he went back to the bathroom to check on Sofia. Looking for a pulse, he found none. Hitting the wall, he let out a loud scream, "No...!" Leonardo came running in with gun in hand as everyone moved out of his way. Once he checked and realized everyone was fine, he stepped out to the hallway to give everyone time to grieve for the dead Sofia. As tears rolled down Giovanni's cheeks, he kept whispering in Italian, "Forgive me, brother." After a little while, Carmelita told Giovanni, "We have to tell Carlos. He has to know." They sent the driver to pick him up. The driver was instructed to only tell Carlos that he was needed at home immediately. When he arrived, Carmelita was by one side and Giovanni by the other. They told him that his mother had a bad reaction to her new medication and that she had passed away. Carlos was in shock. He put his hands over his face and began to weep like a child. Nobody could comfort him. He had lost his mother. His loss was great.

Giovanni made all of the funeral arrangements. Sofia had the most elegant funeral, just as she would have wanted. But only the house staff and the three of them with the baby attended the services. Nobody else came. Evidently no one cared for someone so bad.

A few days after Sofia was buried, Giovanni announced he soon had to go back to his office and attend to all of his businesses. He actually owned a hospital and many clinics. Both Carlos and Carmelita begged him to stay. It didn't take much to change his mind. He was older and had no one to go home to. Giovanni made arrangements to be able to care for his businesses while still being close to his family. He accepted their invitation and retired to be with them. Shortly after, while Giovanni was in the kitchen with Carmelita, teaching her how to make pasta and singing Sicilian's songs to baby Angelo, he had a deadly heart attack. But even in his last moments he was smiling, as if saying, "Don't worry, I'm fine." Unlike Sofia's, his funeral was huge with over three thousand people attending, and most of them were crying for someone who had helped them or saved them, or both. Many undoubtedly loved Uncle Giovanni.

Mom and Dad had me when Angelo was twenty years old. They thought they could not have any more babies, and then I came. From what I hear I was a bundle of joy. But by this time, Mexico had gone into a great depression. Even though we were very rich, my parents struggled to keep the companies open during these hard times. They also opened many kitchens to feed the poor, and soon everything was lost or taken by the government. With a little bit of money left they moved us here to Los Angeles. Only a few months later, Angelo died in an explosion at a warehouse he managed. As soon as father heard the news, he had a stroke and when into a coma; he died that year, leaving Mom and I alone. And here we are. This is our story. I'm proud to be of Mexican-Sicilian decent and to have come from such a lineage of determined, kind, passionate, and smart working people.

Andrew and Sebastian both shouted, "So, Mom, what was the reason? The reason they had to leave Sicily? You never mentioned the reason why?" I answered, "Boys, it was because my grandfather Gino, Carlo and Giovanni's father, got caught stealing a chicken from Mr. Occeli's farm. You see, Occeli was a very rich man and everyone suspected that he was connected to the Mafia." I continued: Occeli sent his son and two others bullies to capture Gino, my grandfather, and beat him up for the chicken he had stolen. On their way to grandpa's house they encountered Carlo, and to them he was good enough to receive the beating for his father's doing. Not knowing what had happened when Carlo was jumped by these men, he defended himself and instead he gave them, including Occeli's son, the beating of their lives.

By the time Carlo made it home with bloody fists from the fight, it was too late. Occeli's men had taken Gino and shot him just outside the house. My grandma Francesca was by his side, crying for her loving husband, who in desperation had stolen a chicken to feed his family. Giovanni was hidden in the bushes nearby and in shock. He was just a little boy. Mr. Occeli was publicly embarrassed that a poor and younger peasant boy had damaged his son's honor. He was the laughingstock of the town. Sicilians are very proud people, so he killed grandpa and launched a vendetta against the men in our family. Knowing that her kids would be killed, my grandma ran to the shore with her boys and gave her land to a fisherman in exchange for him taking the boys to Rome. They left immediately, waving goodbye to their mother, knowing that they would never again see her and the land they love so much. Time passed by and it seemed that the boys had gotten away. They made it all the way to Monterrey, Mexico. But as I have told you, they found Carlo, my grandfather, and he paid with his own life for the beating of Mr. Occeli's son. I guess they forgave Giovanni because he was so young when this happened, and also because two people had already paid with their lives.

You see, Grandpa Carlo had no choice but to run away as far as he could with his younger brother Giovanni to protect their lives. Giovanni got involved in the Mafia to make a deal and make sure that Mr. Occeli's hand would not continue to reach out and kill the future generations of the men in our family. Of course, he also gave his word that there would not be any repercussions on our part. I also heard he paid a lot of money to Occeli to forgive and forget what had happened. He then went on to do business with him. You see, that's how it is done in Sicily.

It had become late and, finishing the story, I kissed the boy's foreheads and sent them to bed. I said to them, "I know it's a lot to think about, but it is the truth and it's our past." I told them I would be in to pray with them later. As I was getting up from the floor, picking up the pillows I saw the junk mail and newspapers on the corner table. I went on to pick them up and noticed that unmarked letter again. I finally sat down and opened the darn thing.

The letter read, "Carmelita, please don't be shocked, but I am a long-lost family member of yours. I have searched the world for you and my sister. I'm your mother's half sister. We shared the same father, Angelo. Father had me years after your mother, when he came back to Sicily. Father told me that I had a sister, and I never lost faith in finding her, I never believed my sister was dead. I used our father's fortune to look for her, and when I located your mom, I cannot express the happiness I felt. My son is writing this letter for me because my English is not too good. I have sent my son to find you, but he will not come to see you until you call him. He will wait for a month at the Beverly Hills Hotel. His room number is #129. His name is Angelo too, like our father and your brother. Please don't be afraid to talk to him. He brings good news. Ask your mom this question: 'What do you want more then anything?' If I know my sister as I think I do, the blood will call and her answer will be, 'To know about my family.' I can give her that and more. I look forward to connecting with you. Signed with Love, Margarita."

I read the letter and, placing it over my heart, I wept and remembered the calls I had been receiving. The boys heard me crying and came running. "What is wrong, Mom?" they asked. I showed Andrew the letter and he read it aloud. Sebastian started jumping. "Mom! Mommy, we have family in Sicily! And they found us!" We hugged and I cried. We made plans to get Mom the next morning and go look for him. There is really no need to mention that none of us could sleep that night.

That very next day we got up early and went to get Mom. We showed her the letter as we hugged and cried again. It was an answer to her prayers. I told Mom that we would go find Angelo right away. I called my job and got the day off. Then we drove to the luxurious Beverly Hills Hotel, and with a little bit of anxiety but a whole lot of excitement, I asked for room #129. "Will you please call Angelo down to the lobby and tell him that his family is waiting for him?" We all stood around with our eyes fixed on the elevators. Fifteen minutes went by, and I went back to the desk and asked, "Did you call him?" The clerk nodded yes and added, "He said he'd be right down." I walked away, thinking maybe he wants to look good and is fixing himself up for us. Then, all of a sudden, one of the elevator doors opened and a handsome, middle-aged man stepped out. He went straight to Mom and said, "You are my Auntie Carmelita." Mom hugged him and began to cry, as did we all. He kissed all of us on both cheeks and told us that he loved us. He told Mom, "I would recognize you anywhere, Auntie. You look just like your mother. We have a picture of her with Grandpa in our living room. He never got over her loss and yours." Then he went on to say to me, "I'm sorry if I scared you with my phone calls." He knelt down and, grabbing both of the boys, said something in Sicilian. Realizing the boys did not understand, he excused himself and said, "You boys are very handsome." After all the hugs and kisses, he invited us for breakfast up in his room. We went up to the top floor. The place was magnificent. He had a butler and a cook waiting for us. As we sat down he told the boys they could have anything that they wanted. He turned to Mom and as they took a seat together said, "Good news, Auntie Carmelita. When Grandpa Angelo came from America, he had a little bit of money. He was a whiz in the business world and he became wealthy again. He is still alive, yet he is very old and would like to meet his oldest daughter as soon as possible." My mom couldn't stop crying. He grabbed Mom's hands and kissed them both. "There, there," he said to Mom. "It's okay, Auntie. We're finally together."

He went on to say, "My mom, your half sister, never gave up on finding you. We have looked and looked for you, but you ended up in Mexico City with Maria. And then you moved again and again, and as soon as we would get a lead, we would lose you again. It was as if there was a wall keeping us from finding you. We would find you and lose you again and again." I said aloud, "Uncle Giovanni. He might have thought they were looking for Dad." Wiping her tears Mom said, "Yes! Poor Uncle, he thought he was protecting us. Instead he kept my family from finding me, bless his heart."

Angelo went on, "We need to leave tomorrow. Grandpa needs to see all of you and give you his blessing. I have got everyone's passports ready." I said, "Wait a minute! How did you do that?" He answered smiling, "Money buys everything, dear cousin. Please don't get angry. There is no time to lose. I have tickets and passports. You don't need anything else." I said, "What about clothing and ...

my toothbrush?" Patiently he said, "You can always buy everything over there."

"My life has been filled with happy and sad events," Mom said. To finally see my father and my sister too … this it's a miracle. A gift from God. What a pleasant dream I'm having today."

When we arrived in Sicily, Mom's sister, Auntie Margarita, greeted us at the airport. The two sisters embraced and there were many tears of joy. Holding each other tightly, they got in the limo and, trying to understand one another, they spoke until we got to the house, which was more like a castle. There, people rushed to our arrival, and Grandpa Angelo in a wheelchair extended his arms to his lost daughter, my mom.

In loving memory of my mom

Note:

To all my readers, thank you for your support and I hope you'll enjoy my upcoming books

About The Author

"Find the courage to follow your dreams and wait for great things to happen"

She has always shared the love of writing that her father had, so, she gives you her thoughts and her soul in black and white, hopping you will find them as wonderful as she thinks they are.

They came to Los Angeles, California, when she was about fourteen years old, right after she lost her dad to Cancer.

With much struggle and hard work her mom and her begin a new life, together they share the good with the bad and survived it all.

She is of Sicilian, Scottish English and Mexican decent, like everyone else she's a Heinz 57.

Printed in the United States
69242LVS00004B/56